Dear Family and Friends of New Readers,

Welcome to Scholastic Reader. We have taken more than eighty years of experience with teachers, parents, and children and put it into a program that is designed to match your child's interest and skills. Each Scholastic Reader is designed to support your child's efforts to learn how to read at every age and every stage.

- First Reader
- Preschool - Kindergarten
- ABC's
- First words

- Beginning Reader
- Preschool - Grade 1
- Sight words
- Words to sound out
- Simple sentences

- Developing Reader
- Grades 1 – 2
- New vocabulary
- Longer sentences

- Growing Reader
- Grades 1 – 3
- Reading for inspiration and information

On the back of every book, we have indicated the grade level, guided reading level, Lexile® level, and word count. You can use this information to find a book that is a good fit for your child.

For ideas about sharing books with your new reader, please visit www.scholastic.com. Enjoy helping your child learn to read and love to read!

Happy Reading!

—**Francie Alexander**
Chief Academic Officer
Scholastic Inc.

Photo Credits:

Front cover: © Victor de Schwanberg / Alamy. **Back cover:** © Galyna Abdrushko / Shutterstock. **Interior:** 3: © Mettefoto / Alamy; 4 – 5: © Ragnarock / Shutterstock; 6 full page © Galyna Abdrushko / Shutterstock; 6 top inset: © MaszaS / Shutterstock; 6 bottom inset: © Paul Banton / Shutterstock; 7: © Oleksiy Maksymenko / Alamy; 8 – 9: © Elnur / Shutterstock; 9 inset: © Juburg / Shutterstock; 10 – 11: © MaxFX / Shutterstock; 12 inset: © National Geographic / Getty Images; 12 – 13: © Terry Andrewartha / Nature Picture Library; 14 – 15: © Gregory Pelt / Shutterstock; 16: © Michael Stevelmans / Shutterstock; 17: © Steve Cole / Photodisc / Getty Images; 18 – 19: © Grant Faint / Photographer's Choice/ Getty Images; 20: © Terrance Emerson / Shutterstock; 21: © Tetra Images / Alamy; 22 – 23: © J. Breedlove / Shutterstock; 23 top inset: © Doug Steley A / Alamy; 23 bottom inset: © Morgan Lane Photography / Shutterstock; 24 – 25: © shalunts / Shutterstock; 25 inset: © Colman Lerner Gerardo / Shutterstock; 27: © Jimmy Lu / Shutterstock; 28: © Saniphoto / Shutterstock; 29: © JUPITERIMAGES / i2i / Alamy; 30 – 31: © Digital Vision / Alamy

ISBN-13: 978-0-545-07231-1
ISBN-10: 0-545-07231-X

Book design: Kay Petronio

Expert reader:
Reviewed by Gordian Raacke, Executive Director,
Renewable Energy Long Island. Mr. Raacke was trained as a
Climate Messenger by Vice President Al Gore and The Climate Project.

12 11 10 9 8 7 6 5 4 3 2   9 10 11 12 13 14/0

Printed in the U.S.A.
First printing, March 2009

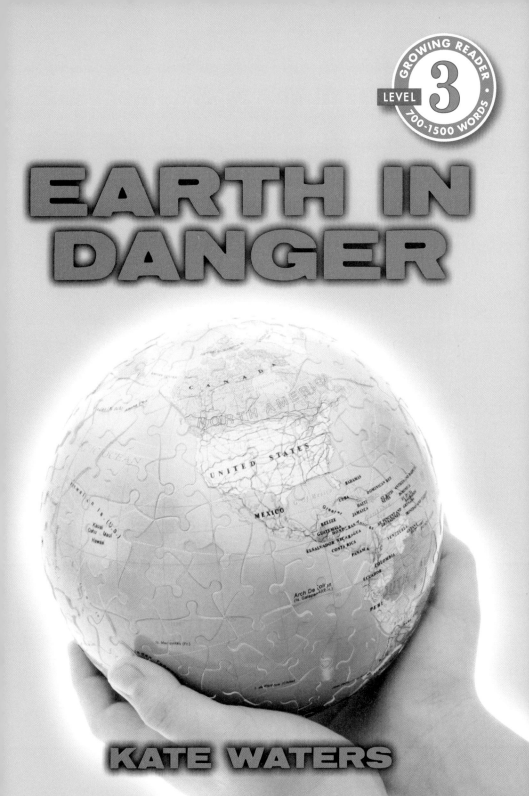

LEVEL 3
GROWING READER · 700-1500 WORDS

EARTH IN DANGER

KATE WATERS

SCHOLASTIC INC.

New York   Toronto   London   Auckland   Sydney
Mexico City   New Delhi   Hong Kong   Buenos Aires

Planet Earth looks beautiful from space. You can see white clouds, blue oceans, brown deserts, and green forests. Other planets are too hot or too cold for living things to survive. Earth is the only planet where they can live.

People, plants, and animals need gases like oxygen and carbon dioxide to live.

Our atmosphere is the mixture of these and other gases that surround Earth. Think of the atmosphere as a blanket that covers Earth. It starts at the ground and reaches up more than thirty miles above Earth.

Living things also need light and heat from the sun. The atmosphere keeps some of the sun's heat near the Earth. But it lets some of the heat go back out to space so Earth does not get too hot.

You can compare the atmosphere to a greenhouse. Sunlight comes in through the glass walls. The air inside the greenhouse gets hot. Some of the hot air escapes through vents. That way the temperature inside the greenhouse is controlled.

Scientists have noticed that our atmosphere is changing. Carbon dioxide and other gases are building up in the atmosphere. Less heat is escaping. Earth is getting hotter. This is called the greenhouse effect.

Some change in the temperature of Earth is natural. Thousands of years ago, Earth was very cold. But Earth gradually got warm again. Scientists think that changes like this have been happening for millions of years. But right now Earth may be heating up too quickly. This is called global warming.

Scientists measure glaciers in mountain valleys and polar regions. They see that many glaciers are melting. That is how they know Earth is getting hotter.

Ice is melting in polar regions. Penguins, polar bears, and other polar animals have less and less ice to live and rest on. The level of the ocean water is rising. Towns along the coasts will flood more easily in a storm.

Scientists have noticed that hurricanes and other tropical storms are getting more powerful. That's because the temperature of ocean water is rising. Hurricanes only form above warm ocean water.

Most scientists think that people are causing these changes. We burn fossil fuels when we ride in our cars, heat our homes, or use electricity.

Burning fossil fuels increases the amount of carbon dioxide in the atmosphere. That makes the atmosphere reflect more heat back to Earth. Less heat can escape, so Earth warms up.

You may have heard about carbon footprints. That is a term for how much carbon dioxide we put in the atmosphere each day. Every year there are more and more people on Earth. Our carbon footprint is getting bigger and bigger.

People all over the world are working to reduce the amount of fossil fuels we burn. They are finding new sources of energy that do not put carbon dioxide into the atmosphere. Some new cars use both gas and electricity. Solar panels use energy from sunlight to power houses and offices. Windmills can create energy, too.

People are also trying to use less energy. Special light bulbs use less energy than regular bulbs. Many people try to use less heat in winter and less air conditioning in summer.

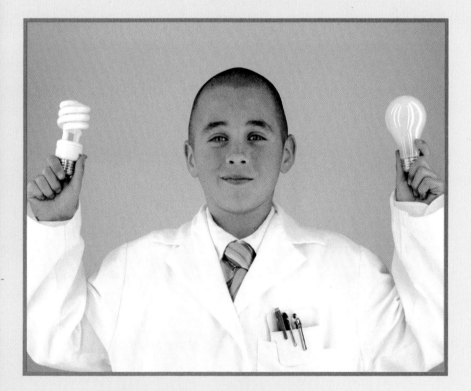

Did you know that our trash can create a gas that thickens the greenhouse gases in the atmosphere? Recycling glass, paper, and aluminum can help. Reusing objects reduces the amount of trash we make.

Plastic bags can't be recycled. Many people are using reusable cloth shopping bags.

PUT AN END TO PLASTIC BAGS

WE RECYCLE

Our atmosphere depends on plants and trees. They change carbon dioxide into oxygen that we need to breathe.

People are cutting down forests for lumber in some parts of the world. They are also clearing land for farms. That is called deforestation. It's another cause of global warming.

To help, we need to plant new trees. We can also use wood from plants that grow fast, such as bamboo, for floors and furniture. These plants grow back more quickly than old, slow-growing trees.

We can also help by not wasting good food. Reducing waste will mean that fewer trees will have to be cut down to grow food crops.

People are trying to reduce their carbon footprints. Here are some things you can do:

- Turn off the lights when you leave a room.

- Keep the refrigerator door closed while deciding what to eat.

- Turn off the TV when you are not watching.

- Carpool or ride your bike to save gas.

- Ask your parents if you can plant a tree in your yard.

- Don't take more food than you can eat.

- Recycle everything you can.

All over the world, people are thinking about the big and small things they can do to keep the planet healthy. Governments are trying to reduce burning fossil fuels. Towns are starting recycling programs. People are planting gardens to grow their own food.

Every little thing we do will help Earth's atmosphere. We will be helping Earth support life for many, many years.

Glossary

carbon—a chemical element found in all fossil fuels, plants, and animals

carbon dioxide—a gas that is released when we burn fossil fuels. Plants absorb it. People and animals breathe it out.

carbon footprint—a measure of how much fuel people use, and how much it impacts the environment

fossil fuel—coal, oil, or natural gas, formed deep in the Earth

gas—a substance, such as air, that will spread to fill any space

oxygen—a colorless gas found in the air, which humans and animals need to breathe

polar regions—the icy areas around the North and South Poles

space—the universe beyond the Earth's atmosphere

tropical—to do with the hot, rainy area near the equator

vent—an opening through which air, smoke, or fumes can escape